THE 3:16® PROMISE

MAX LUCADO

THOMAS NELSON
Since 1798

NASHVILLE DALLAS MEXICO CITY RIO DE JANEIRO

Published in Nashville, Tennessee, by Thomas Nelson. Thomas Nelson is a registered trademark of Thomas Nelson, Inc.

Thomas Nelson, Inc. books may be purchased in bulk for educational, business, fund-raising, or sales promotional use. For information, please e-mail SpecialMarkets@ThomasNelson.com.

All material is adapted from *3:16: The Numbers of Hope.*

ISBN 978-0-8499-1919-0

Printed in the United States of America
11 12 13 14 QG 20 19 18

CONTENTS

1

A PARADE OF HOPE

It's the Hope Diamond of the Bible.

For God
so loved the world
that he gave his one and only Son,
that whoever believes in him
shall not perish but have
eternal life.

A twenty-six-word parade of hope: beginning with God, ending with life, and urging us to do the same. Brief enough to write on a napkin or memorize in a moment, yet solid enough to weather two thousand years of storms and questions. If you know nothing of the Bible, start here. If you know everything in the Bible, return here. We all need the reminder. The heart of the human problem is the heart of the human. And God's treatment is prescribed in John 3:16.

He loves.

He gave.

We believe.

We live.

The words are to Scripture what the Mississippi River is to America—an entryway into the Heartland. Believe or dismiss them, embrace or reject them, any serious consideration of Christ must include them. Would a British historian dismiss the Magna Carta? Egyptologists overlook the

Rosetta Stone? Could you ponder the words of Christ and never immerse yourself into John 3:16?

The verse is an alphabet of grace, a table of contents to the Christian hope, each word a safe-deposit box of jewels. Read it again, slowly and aloud, and note the word that snatches your attention. "For God so loved the world that he gave his one and only Son, that whoever believes in him shall not perish but have eternal life."

"God so *loved* the world . . ." We'd expect an anger-fueled God. One who punishes the world, recycles the world, forsakes the world . . . but loves the world?

The *world*? This world? Heartbreakers, hope-snatchers and dream-dousers prowl this orb. Dictators rage. Abusers inflict. Reverends think they deserve the title. But God loves. And he loves the world so much he gave his:

Declarations?

Rules?

Dicta?

Edicts?

No. The heart-stilling, mind-bending, deal-making-or-breaking claim of John 3:16 is this: *God gave his Son . . . his only Son.* No abstract ideas, but a flesh-wrapped divinity. Scripture equates Jesus with God. God, then, gave himself. Why? So that "*whoever* believes in him shall not perish."

2

GOD LOVES

Pluto got bumped, cut from the first team, demoted from the top nine. According to a committee of scientists meeting in Prague, this outpost planet fails to meet solar-system standards. They downgraded the globe to asteroid #134340.[1] Believe me, Pluto was not happy. I caught up with the dissed sky traveler at a popular constellation hangout, The Night Sky Lounge.

MAX: Tell me, Pluto, how do you feel about the decision of the committee?

PLUTO: You mean those planet-pickers from Prague?

MAX: Yes.

PLUTO: I say no planet is perfect. Mars looks like a tanning bed addict. Saturn has rings around the collar, and Jupiter moons everyone who passes.

MAX: So you don't approve of the decision?

PLUTO: (*Snarling and whipping out a newspaper*) Who comes up with these rules? *Too small. Wrong size moon. Not enough impact.* Do they know how hard it is to hang on at the edge of the solar system? They think I'm spacey—let them duck meteors at thousands of miles per hour for a few millennia, and then see who they call a planet. I'm outta here. I can take the hint. I know when I'm not wanted. Walt Disney named a dog after me. Teachers always put me last on the science quiz. Darth Vader gives me more respect. I'm joining up with a meteor shower. Tell that committee to keep an eye on the night sky. I know where they live.

Can't fault Pluto for being ticked. One day he's in, the next he's out; one day on the squad, the next off. We can understand his frustration. Some of us understand it all too well. We know what it's like to be voted out. Wrong size. Wrong color. Wrong address.

Plutoed.

To the demoted and demeaned, Jesus directs his leadoff verb. "For God so *loved* the world . . ." *Love.* We've all but worn out the word. This morning I used *love* to describe my feelings toward my wife and toward peanut butter. Far from identical emotions. I've never proposed to a jar of peanut butter (though I have let one sit on my lap during a television show). Overuse has defused the word, leaving it with the punch of a butterfly wing.

Compare our love with God's? Look at the round belly of the pregnant peasant girl in Bethlehem. God's in there; the same God who can balance the universe on the tip of his finger floats in Mary's womb. Why? Love.

Peek through the Nazareth workshop window. See the lanky lad sweeping the sawdust from the floor? He once blew stardust into the night sky. Why swap the heavens for a carpentry shop? One answer: love.

Love explains why he came.

Love explains how he endured.

His hometown kicked him out. A so-called friend turned him in. Hucksters called God a hypocrite. Sinners called God guilty. Do termites mock an eagle, tapeworms decry the beauty of a swan? How did Jesus endure such derision? "For God so loved . . ."

"Observe how Christ loved us. . . . He didn't love in order to get something from us but to give everything of himself to us" (Eph. 5:2 MSG).

Your goodness can't win God's love. Nor can your badness lose it. But you can resist it. We tend to do so honestly. Having been Plutoed so often, we fear God may Pluto us as well. Rejections have left us skittish and jumpy. Like my dog Salty.

He sleeps next to me on the couch as I write. He's a cranky cuss, but I like him. We've aged together over the last fifteen years, and he seems worse for the wear. He's a wiry canine by nature; shave his salt-and-pepper mop, and he'd pass for a bulimic Chihuahua. He didn't have much to start with; now the seasons have taken his energy, teeth, hearing, and all but eighteen inches' worth of eyesight.

Toss him a dog treat, and he just stares at

the floor through cloudy cataracts. (Or, in his case, dogaracts?) He's nervous and edgy, quick to growl and slow to trust. As I reach out to pet him, he yanks back. Still, I pet the old coot. I know he can't see, and I can only wonder how dark his world has become.

We are a lot like Salty. I have a feeling that most people who defy and deny God do so more out of fear than conviction. For all our chest pumping and braggadocio, we are an anxious folk—can't see a step into the future, can't hear the one who owns us. No wonder we try to gum the hand that feeds us.

But God reaches and touches. He speaks through the immensity of the Russian plain and the density of the Amazon rain forest. Through a physician's touch in Africa, a bowl of rice in India. Through a Japanese bow or a South American *abraço*. He's even been known to touch people through paragraphs like the ones you are reading. If he is touching you, let him.

Mark it down: God loves you with an unearthly love. You can't win it by being winsome. You can't lose it by being a loser.

God will not let you go. He has handcuffed himself to you in love. And he owns the only key. You need not win his love. You already have it. And, since you can't win it, you can't lose it.

Others demote you. God claims you. Let the definitive voice of the universe say, "You're still a part of my plan."

3

GOD GAVE

As far as medical exams are concerned, this one was simple. As far as I'm concerned, no exam is simple if it couples the word *irregular* with *heartbeat*. I knew I was prone to have an accelerated pulse. When I see Denalyn, my ticker ramps up. When Denalyn brings me a bowl of ice cream, you'd think a Geiger counter had struck pay dirt in my chest.

Such palpitations are to be expected. It was the random rhythms that concerned the cardiologist. You won't find a kinder physician. He did his best to assure me that, as far as heart conditions go, mine isn't serious: "When it comes to cardiac concerns, you've got the best kind."

Forgive my anemic enthusiasm. But isn't that like telling the about-to-leap paratrooper: "Your parachute has a defect, but it's not the worst type"? I prefer the treatment of another heart doctor. He saw my condition and made this eye-popping offer: "Let's exchange hearts. Mine is sturdy; yours is frail. Mine pure, yours diseased. Take mine and enjoy its vigor. Give me yours. I'll endure its irregularity."

Where do you find such a physician? You can reach him at this number—3:16. At the heart of this verse, he deals with the heart of our problem: "For God so loved the world that he *gave* his one and only Son."

"That's the craziest claim I've ever

heard," a man once told me. He and I shared a row and a meal on an airplane. But we did not share an appreciation for John 3:16.

"I don't need God to *give* anyone for me," he claimed. "I've led a good life. Held a good job. People respect me. My wife loves me. I don't need God to give me his son."

Perhaps you agree. You appreciate the teachings of Jesus. Admire his example. But no matter how you turn it around, you can't see the significance of his death. How can the death of Christ mean life for us? The answer begins with a heart exam.

"The heart is deceitful above all things, and desperately wicked" (Jer. 17:9 NKJV). The Spiritual Cardiologist scans our hearts and finds deep disease: "For from within, out of men's hearts, come evil thoughts, sexual immorality, theft, murder, adultery, greed, malice, deceit, lewdness, envy, slander, arrogance and folly" (Mark 7:21–22).

He describes our problem in pandemic proportions. "No one is righteous—not even one. No one is truly wise; no one is seeking God" (Rom. 3:10–11 NLT).

Surely this is an overstatement, an exaggeration. Can it be that "we are utterly incapable of living the glorious lives God wills for us" (Rom. 3:23 MSG)?

This generation is oddly silent about sin. Late-night talk shows don't discuss humanity's shortcomings. Some mental health professionals mock our need for divine forgiveness. At the same time we rape the earth, squander nonrenewable resources, and let 24,000 people die daily from hunger or hunger-related causes.[2] In these "modern" decades we have invented global threat, reinvented genocide and torture. The twentieth century saw more slaughters than any other century in history.[3]

Barbarism apparently is alive and well on the planet Earth. Deny our sin? Quasimodo could more easily deny his hump.

Contrast your heart with Christ's. When you list the claims that qualify him as either crazy or kingly, don't omit this one: he asserted to have the only sinless heart in all of history. He invited, "Can any one of you convict me of a single misleading word, a single sinful act?" (John 8:46 MSG). Issue that challenge to my friends, and hands will wave like stalks in a Kansas wheat field. In response to Jesus's challenge, however, no one could convict him of sin. His enemies drummed up false charges in order to arrest him. Pilate, the highest-ranking official in the region, found no guilt in Jesus. Peter, who walked in Jesus's shadow for three years, recorded: "He never did one thing wrong. Not once said anything amiss" (1 Pet. 2:22 MSG).

Jesus's standard mutes all boasting.

So how does he respond to our unholy hearts? Can a good cardiologist spot irregularity and dismiss it? Can God overlook our sin as innocent mistakes? No. He is the one and only judge. He issues decrees, not opinions; commands, not suggestions. They are truth. They emerge from his holy self. Violate them and you dethrone him—dethrone him at the highest cost.

Jesus made his position clear: "Anyone whose life is not holy will never see the Lord" (Heb. 12:14 NCV). Hard-hearted souls will not populate heaven.

It is the "pure in heart" who will "see God" (Matt. 5:8). So where does that leave us? It leaves us drawing hope from a five-letter Greek word.

Hyper means "in place of" or "on behalf of."[4] New Testament writers repeatedly turned to this preposition to describe the work of Christ:

"Christ died for [*hyper*] our sins . . ." (1 Cor. 15:3).

"Jesus gave himself for [*hyper*] our sins" (Gal. 1:4 NCV).

"Christ redeemed us from the curse of the Law, having become a curse for [*hyper*] us" (Gal. 3:13 NASB).

For sounding hyper about *hyper*, I apologize, but the point is crucial. Christ exchanged hearts with you. Yes, your thieving, lying, adulterous, and murderous heart. He placed your sin in himself and invited God to punish it. "The LORD has put on him the punishment for all the evil we have done" (Isa. 53:6 NCV).

A Chinese Christian understood this point. Before her baptism, a pastor asked a question to ensure she understood the meaning of the cross. "Did Jesus have any sin?" he inquired.

"Oh, yes," she replied.

Troubled, he repeated the question.

"He had sin," she answered positively.

The leader set out to correct her, but she insisted, "He had mine."[5]

Though healthy, Jesus took our disease

upon himself. Though diseased, we who accept his offer are pronounced healthy. More than pardoned, we are declared innocent. We enter heaven, not with healed hearts, but with his heart. It is as if we have never sinned. Read slowly the announcement of Paul: "If anyone is in Christ, he is a new creation; the old has gone, the new has come!" (2 Cor. 5:17).

This is no transplant, mind you, but a swap. The holy and the vile exchange locations. God makes healthy what is sick, right what is wrong, straight what was crooked.

Scarred and journey-hardened we come. "Can you do something with this heart?" we ask.

He nods and smiles. "Suppose we discuss a swap."

4

WE BELIEVE

"Tell me my part again," I groaned.

"Just trust me," she assured. *She* was a bubbly, college-aged, baseball-capped, rope holder. *Trust me* translated into a backward leap off a fifty-foot cliff, wearing a belay harness and a what-did-I-get-myself-into expression.

Some people love rappelling. They relish the stomach-in-the-throat sensation. Not me. I prefer the seat-in-the-chair one. I had traveled to Colorado to experience a week of rest to the fullest. Fresh air, great views. Good coffee, long talks. These events made my list. Half-gainers off the mountain didn't.

Blame persuasive friends and stupid pride for my presence on the peak. The platform team assured me of a safe landing.

"Ever done this?" the girl asked.

"No."

She handed me a leather harness and told me to step in. "It's kind of like a diaper" she smiled, all too chipper. *I may need a diaper*, I thought.

"What about you?" I inquired. "Have you lowered anyone down the mountain?"

"Been working here all summer," she beamed.

It was barely July.

"It's simple," she continued as she clipped me in and handed me gloves. "Hold the rope and jump. Bounce off the wall with your feet."

Someone make a law: the words *jump*, *bounce*, and *wall* should never be spoken in the same breath.

"How do I keep from crashing?"

"You don't. I do that."

"You?"

"Yes, I hold your rope."

Little comfort. Not only was she half my age, she was half my size—more of the ballet than the belay sort. "But don't I do *something?*" I begged.

"You trust me."

I inched up to the edge of the cliff and looked down. Frodo felt safer looking into the pit.

"Do you have any valuables?" I heard a voice ask.

"Only my life."

"You're funny," she chirped, sounding so much like my daughters that I remembered my will was out of date. "Come on. It's your turn!"

I gave her one more look. A look akin

to the one the 3:16 promise often prompts. Can I really trust that "whoever *believes* in him shall not perish"?

Jesus's invitation seems too simple. We gravitate to other verbs. *Work* has a better ring to it. "Whoever works for him will be saved." *Satisfy* fits nicely. "Whoever satisfies him will be saved." But believe? *Shouldn't I do more?*

"Everyone who believes in him will have eternal life" (John 3:15 NLT).

The simplicity troubles many people. We'd expect a more complicated cure, a more elaborate treatment. We expect a more proactive assignment, to have to conjure up a remedy for our sin. Some mercy seekers have donned hair shirts, climbed cathedral steps on their knees, or traversed hot rocks on bare feet.

Others of us have written our own Bible verse: "God helps those who help themselves" (Popular Opinion 1:1). We'll fix ourselves, thank you. We'll make up for our mistakes with contributions, our guilt with busyness. We'll overcome failures with hard work. We'll find salvation the old-fashioned way: we'll earn it.

Christ, in contrast, says to us what the rope-holding girl said to me: "Your part is to trust. Trust me to do what you can't."

By the way, you take similar steps of trust daily, even hourly. You believe the chair will support you, so you set your weight on it. You believe water will hydrate you, so you swallow it. You trust the work of the light switch, so you flip it. You have faith the doorknob will work, so you turn it.

You regularly trust power you cannot see to do a work you cannot accomplish. Jesus invites you to do the same with him.

Just him.

Some historians clump Christ with Moses, Muhammed, Confucius, and other spiritual leaders. But Jesus refuses to share the page. He declares, "I am the way, and the truth, and the life; no one comes to the

Father, but by me" (John 14:6 RSV). He could have scored more points in political correctness had he said, "I *know* the way," or "I *show* the way." Yet, he speaks not of what he does but of who he is: I *am* the way.

His followers refused to soften or shift the spotlight. Peter announced: "There is salvation in no one else! God has given no other name under heaven by which we must be saved" (Acts 4:12 NLT).

Many recoil at such definitiveness. John 14:6 and Acts 4:12 sound primitive in this era of broadbands and broad minds. The world is shrinking, cultures are blending, borders are bending; this is the day of inclusion. All roads lead to heaven, right?

But can they? The sentence makes good talk-show fodder, but is it accurate? Can all approaches to God be correct?

Islam says Jesus was not crucified. Christians say he was. Both can't be right.

Judaism refuses the claim of Christ as

the Messiah.[6] Christians accept it. Someone's making a mistake.

Buddhists look toward Nirvana, achieved after no less than 547 reincarnations.[7] Christians believe in one life, one death, and an eternity of enjoying God. Doesn't one view exclude the other?

Humanists do not acknowledge a creator of life. Jesus claims to be the source of life. One of the two speaks folly.

Spiritists read your palms. Christians consult the Bible.

Hindus perceive a plural and impersonal God.[8] Christ-followers believe "there is only one God" (1 Cor. 8:4 NLT). Somebody is wrong.

And, most supremely, every non-Christian religion says, "You can save you." Jesus says, "My death on the cross saves you."

How can all religions lead to God when they are so different? We don't tolerate such illogic in other matters. We don't pretend that all roads lead to London or all ships sail to Australia. All flights don't land in Rome. Imagine your response to a travel agent who claims they do. You tell him you need a flight to Rome, Italy, so he looks on his screen.

"Well, there is a flight to Sidney, Australia, departing at 6:00 a.m."

"Does it go to Rome?"

"No, but it offers wonderful in-flight dining and movies."

"But I need to go to Rome."

"Then let me suggest Southwest Airlines."

"Southwest Airlines flies to Rome?"

"No, but they have consistently won awards for on-time arrivals."

You're growing frustrated. "I need one airline to carry me to one place: Rome."

The agent appears offended. "Sir, all flights go to Rome."

You know better. Different flights have different destinations. That's not a thickheaded conclusion but an honest one. Every flight does not go to Rome. Every path does not lead to God. Jesus blazed a stand-alone trail void of self-salvation. He cleared a one-of-a-kind passageway uncluttered by human effort. Christ came, not for the strong, but for the weak; not for the righteous, but for the sinner. We enter his way upon confession of our need, not completion of our deeds. He offers a unique-to-him invitation in which he works and we trust, he dies and we live, he invites and we believe.

We believe *in him*. "The work God wants you to do is this: Believe the One he sent" (John 6:29 NCV).

Believe in yourself? No. Believe in him.

Just him. Look to Jesus . . . and believe.

Remember my rappelling partner? She told me to fix my gaze on her. As I took the plunge she shouted, "Keep your eyes up here!" I didn't have to be told twice. She was the only one of the two of us smiling.

But since she did her work, I landed safely. Next trip, however, you'll find me in a chair on the porch.

5

WE LIVE

A friend from my West Texas hometown contacted me with some big news. "My father saw your mother's name in an unclaimed property column of the local newspaper."

I couldn't imagine what the property might be. Dad died years ago. Mom lives near my sister in Arkansas. We sold her house. As far as I knew, we owned nothing in the city. "Unclaimed property?"

"Sure, city hall is obliged to list the names of folks who own these goods."

"You don't say."

"I'll send you the contact information."

That was on Sunday. His e-mail arrived on Tuesday. That left me the better part of forty-eight hours to imagine what my folks, unbeknownst to their kids, had hoarded away. Initially, I was stumped. The Great Depression honed my parents into penny pinchers. They did to dollars what boa constrictors do to rats—squeezed the life out of them.

Then again, Dad worked as an oil-field mechanic. Wildcatters roam such parts. Did one convince him to quietly invest a few bucks in a long-shot oil well? Did he keep it from Mom lest she erupt? And now, could it be that the well has oil? A petroleum gusher might mean millions, no, zillions of barrels of black gold flowing from the Devonian treasure. And who is listed among the investors but Jack Lucado. And who is listed among his heirs?

My imagination raced like a Formula One driver. *This could be big.* By Sunday evening I'd funded my yet-to-be-born grandchildren's education. On Monday I ended world hunger. Tuesday, as the e-mail came, I was solving the AIDS crisis. I dialed the courthouse number. The clerk remembered my mom and, with no small enthusiasm, affirmed, "I've been hoping you'd call." I heard papers shuffling, her voice mumbling, "Now where did I put that check?"

Check? Gulp. I pulled a calculator out of my desk and limbered my fingers. "Here it is," she exclaimed, speaking back into the phone. "Looks like we owe your mom some money. Whoa, this has been here awhile."

I drummed my fingers on the desk.

"Let's see, Mr. Lucado. Where should we send this check?"

I gave her an address and waited.

She continued. "Looks like we owe your mom three fifty."

Did she say th-th-three hundred and fifty million? I collected myself. She might mean thousand. *Whichever, way to go, Dad.*

"Yes, sir, your mother overpaid her final water bill by three dollars and fifty cents. Shall I send that today?

"Sure . . . thanks. Just put it in the mail."

Some hopes fail to deliver. Some expectations sputter and flop like an untied balloon. Remember the shining-armor boyfriend who became the heartbreaking two-timer? The fast-track promotion that landed you in the forgotten basement cubicle? The cross-country move you made to "find yourself"? You found yourself, all right. You found yourself with higher rent and fewer friends.

"If only" dreams lurk in each biography. "If only I could find a mate . . . a career . . . a bright red, affordable '65 Mustang." The only barrier between you and bliss is an "if only." Sometimes you cross it. You find the mate or the career or the Mustang and . . . you count the three fifty and sigh.

Life has letdowns. And how do you know Christ won't be one of them? Honestly. Dare you believe that he gives what he promises to give? Life. Eternal life. "Whoever believes in him shall not perish but have eternal life" (John 3:16).

Beer companies offer you life in their hops. Perfume makers promise new life for your romance. But don't confuse costume jewelry with God's sapphire.

Jesus offers *zoe*, the Greek word for "life as God has it."[9] Whereas *bios*, its sibling term, is life extensive, *zoe* is life intensive. Jesus talks less about life's duration and more about its quality, vitality, energy, and fulfillment. What the new mate, sports car, or unexpected check could never do, Christ says, "I can." You'll love how he achieves it. He reconnects your soul with God.

What God gave Adam and Eve, he entrusted to you and me. A soul. "The LORD God formed man of the dust of the ground, and breathed into his nostrils the breath of life; and man became a living being" (Gen. 2:7 NKJV).

You, a bipedal ape? Chemical fluke? Atomic surprise? By no means. You bear the very breath of God. He exhaled himself into you, making you a "living being" (v. 7).

Your soul distinguishes you from zoo dwellers. God gifted the camel with a hump and the giraffe with a flagpole neck, but he reserved his breath, or a soul, for you. You bear his stamp. You do things God does. Think. Question. Reflect. You blueprint buildings, chart sea crossings, and swallow throat lumps when your kids say their alphabet. You, like Adam, have a soul.

And, like Adam, you've used your soul to disobey God. God's command to the charter couple includes the Bible's first reference to death. "You must not eat from the tree of the knowledge of good and evil, for when you eat of it you will surely die" (v. 17).

My daughter Andrea, when elementary-school age, asked a grown-up question. "Dad, if God didn't want them to eat from the tree, why did he put it there?" The answer, best I can tell, is to remind us who created whom. When we attempt to swap roles with God and tell him we can eat (think, say, do, control, own, hurt, inhale, ingest, demand) anything we want, we die two deaths. Adam and Eve did. They died physically, eventually, and spiritually, instantly.

Reread God's warning: "*when* you eat of it you will surely die" (v. 17). Sin resulted in Adam and Eve's immediate deaths. But death of what? Their bodies? No, they continued to breathe. Brain waves flowed. Eyelids blinked. Their bodies functioned, but their hearts hardened. They stopped trusting God. Their friendship with their maker died.

We understand how this happened. If

you loan me your car and I wreck it, will I want to see you again? No. I will dread our next encounter. Adam and Eve experienced the same.

Prior to this act, they followed God like sheep follow their shepherd. He spoke; they listened. He gave assignments; they fulfilled them. They were naked but unashamed, transparent and unafraid. Yet as one drop of ink clouds a glass of water, the stubborn deed darkened their souls. Everything changed. God's presence stirred panic, not peace. Adam ran like a kid caught raiding the pantry. "I was afraid" (Gen. 3:10). Intimacy with God ceased; separation from God began. We'll always wonder why Adam didn't ask for forgiveness. But he didn't, and the guilty pair was "banished . . . from the Garden of Eden" (Gen. 3:23).

We've loitered outside the gates ever since.

Deep within we've known (haven't we known?) something is awry—we feel disconnected. What we hope will bring life, brings limited amounts . . . three fifty worth. We connect with a career, find meaning in family, yet long for something more.

We feel the frustration I felt on Christmas morning, 1964. I assembled a nine-year-old's dream gift: a genuine Santa Fe Railroad miniature train set, complete with battery-powered engine and flashing crossing lights. I placed the locomotive on the tracks and watched in sheer glee as three pounds of pure steel wound its way across my bedroom floor. Around and around and around and . . . around . . . and around . . . After some time I picked it up and turned it the other direction. It went around and around and around . . .

"Mom, what else did you get me for Christmas?"

Similarly, our lives chug in long ovals, one lap after another. First job. Promotion. Wedding day. Nursery beds. Kids. Grandkids. Around and around . . . Is there anything else?

Our dissatisfaction mates with disappointment and gives birth to some unruly children: drunkenness, power plays, eighty-hour workweeks, nosedives into sexual perversions—nothing more than poorly disguised longings for Eden. We long to restore what Adam lost. As someone once said, "The man who knocks on the door of a brothel is seeking God."

Where and when the brothel fails, Jesus steps forth with a reconnection invitation. Though we be "dead in [our] transgressions and sins (Eph. 2:1) and separated from the life of God (Eph. 4:18), whoever believes that Jesus is the Christ is born of God. (1 John 5:1 NKJV) Reborn! This is not a physical birth resulting from human passion or plan—this rebirth comes from God" (John 1:13 NLT).

Don't miss the invisible, inward miracle triggered by belief. God reinstates us to Garden-of-Eden status. What Adam and Eve did, we now do! The flagship family walked with God; we can too. They heard his voice; so can we. They were naked and unashamed; we can be transparent and unafraid. No more running or hiding.

His offer still stands. "Because Jesus was raised from the dead, we've been given a brand-new life and have everything to live for, including a future in heaven—and the future starts now!" (1 Pet. 1:3–4 MSG).

Others offer life, but no one offers to do what Jesus does—to reconnect us to his power. But how can we know? How do we know that Jesus knows what he's talking about? The ultimate answer, according to his flagship followers, is the vacated tomb. Did you note the words you just read? "Because Jesus was *raised from the dead*, we've been given a brand-new life." In the final sum, it was the disrupted grave that convinced the maiden Christians to cast their lots with Christ. "He was seen by Peter and then by the twelve apostles. After that, Jesus was seen by more than five hundred believers at the same time" (1 Cor. 15:5–6 NCV).

Can Jesus actually replace death with life? He did a convincing job with his own. We can trust him because he has been there.

On a trip to China I rode past Tiananmen Square in a bus full of Westerners. We tried to recollect the causes and consequences of the revolt. Our knowledge of history was embarrassing. One gave one date; another gave a different one. One person remembered a certain death toll; someone else disagreed. All this time our translator remained silent.

Finally one of us asked her, "Do you remember anything about the Tiananmen Square revolt?"

Her answer was solemn. "Yes, I was a part of it."

We quickly grew quiet as she gave first-hand recollections of the bloodshed and oppression. We listened, because she'd been there.

We who follow Christ do so for the same reason. He's been there . . .

He's been to Bethlehem, wearing barn rags and hearing sheep crunch. Suckling milk and shivering against the cold. All of divinity content to cocoon itself in an eight-pound body and to sleep on a cow's supper. Millions who face the chill of empty pockets or the fears of sudden change turn to Christ. Why?

Because he's been there.

He's been to Nazareth, where he made deadlines and paid bills; to Galilee, where he recruited direct reports and separated fighters; to Jerusalem, where he stared down critics and stood up against cynics.

We have our Nazareths as well—demands and due dates. Jesus wasn't the last to build a team; accusers didn't disappear with Jerusalem's temple. Why seek Jesus's help with your challenges? Because he's been there. To Nazareth, to Galilee, to Jerusalem.

But most of all, he's been to the grave. Not as a visitor, but as a corpse. Buried amidst the cadavers. Numbered among the dead. Heart silent and lungs vacant. Body wrapped and grave sealed. The cemetery. He's been buried there.

You haven't, yet. But you will be. And since you will, don't you need someone who knows the way out?

"God . . . has given us new birth into a living hope through the resurrection of Jesus Christ from the dead" (1 Pet. 1:3 NIV). "He destroyed death, and through the Good News he showed us the way to have life that cannot be destroyed" (1 Pet. 1:3 NIV; 2 Tim. 1:10 NCV).

Remember that check from my hometown? I'm still waiting on it. Not counting on it for much. The three fifty promises to bring little. But the 3:16 promise? I've long since deposited that check. It bears interest every day and will forever.

Yours will too.

6

THE INVITATION

Two of our three daughters were born in the South Zone of Rio de Janeiro, Brazil. We lived in the North Zone, separated from our doctor's office and hospital by a tunnel-pierced mountain range. During Denalyn's many months of pregnancy, we made the drive often.

We didn't complain. Signs of life do a samba on every street corner. Copacabana and her bathers. Ipanema and her coffee bars. Gavea and her glamour. We never begrudged the South Zone forays. But they sure did bewilder me. I kept getting lost. I'm directionally challenged anyway, prone to take a wrong turn between the bedroom and bathroom. Complicate my disorientation with randomly mapped three-hundred-year-old streets, and I don't stand a chance.

I had one salvation. Jesus. Literally, Jesus. The Christ the Redeemer statue. The figure stands guard over the city, one hundred and twenty-five feet tall with an arm span of nearly a hundred feet. More than a thousand tons of reinforced steel. The head alone measures ten feet from chin to scalp. Perched a mile and a half above sea level on Corcovado Mountain, the elevated Jesus is always visible. Especially to those who are looking for it. Since I was often lost, I was often looking. As a sailor seeks land, I searched for the statue, peering between the phone lines and rooftops for the familiar friendly face. Find him and find my bearings.

John 3:16 offers you an identical promise. The verse elevates Christ to thin-air loftiness, crowning him with the most regal of titles: "One and Only Son."

Jesus enjoys an intimacy with God, a mutuality the Father shares with no one else. He "exists at the very heart of the Father" (John 1:18 MSG).

When Jesus says, "In my Father's house are many mansions" (John 14:2 NKJV), count on it. He knows. He has walked them.

When he says, "You are worth more than many sparrows" (Matt. 10:31), trust him. Jesus knows. He knows the value of every creature.

When Christ declares, "Your Father knows what you need" (Matt. 6:8 NAB), believe it. After all, "He was in the beginning with God" (John 1:2 NAB).

Heaven's door has onc key, and Jesus holds it.

Think of it this way. You're a fifth grader studying astronomy. The day you read about the first mission to the moon, you and your classmates pepper the teacher with space-travel questions.

"What does moon dust feel like?"

"Can you swallow when there's no gravity?"

"What about going to the bathroom?"

The teacher does the best she can but prefaces most replies with "I would guess . . ." or "I think . . ." or "Perhaps . . ."

How could she know? She's never been there. But the next day she brings a guest who has. Neil Armstrong enters the room. Yes, the "one small step for man, one giant leap for mankind" Neil Armstrong.

"Now ask your questions," the teacher invites. And Astronaut Armstrong answers each with certainty. He knows the moon; he's walked on it. No speculation or hesitation—he speaks with conviction.

So did Jesus. "He was teaching them as

one who had authority" (Matt. 7:29 ESV). Jesus knows the dimensions of God's throne room, the fragrance of its incense, the favorite songs of the unceasing choir. He has a unique, one-of-a-kind, unrivaled knowledge of God and wants to share his knowledge with you. "No one truly knows the Father except the Son and those *to whom the Son chooses to reveal him*" (Matt. 11:27 NLT).

Jesus doesn't boast in his knowledge; he shares it. He doesn't gloat; he gives. He doesn't revel; he reveals. He reveals to us the secrets of eternity.

And he shares them, not just with the top brass or purebred, but with the hungry and needy. In the very next line, Jesus invites: "Come to me, all of you who are weary and carry heavy burdens, and I will give you rest. Take my yoke upon you. Let me teach you, because I am humble and gentle at heart, and you will find rest for your souls" (vv. 28–29 NLT).

Do yourself a favor. Find the brightest highlighter manufactured and the darkest ink produced. Underscore, underline, and accept his invitation: "Let me teach you . . ."

One of my Boy Scout assignments was to build a kite. One of my blessings as a Boy Scout was a kite-building dad. He built a lot of things: scooters on skates, go-carts. Why, he even built our house. A kite to him was stick figures to Van Gogh. Could handle them in his sleep.

With wood glue, poles, and newspaper, we fashioned a sky-dancing masterpiece: red, white, and blue, and shaped like a box. We launched our creation on the back of a March wind. But after some minutes, my kite caught a downdraft and plunged. I tightened the string, raced in reverse, and did all I could to maintain elevation. But it was too late. She Hindenburged earthward.

Envision a red-headed, heartsick twelve-year-old standing over his collapsed kite.

That was me. Envision a square-bodied man with ruddy skin and coverall, placing his hand on the boy's shoulder. That was my kite-making dad. He surveyed the heap of sticks and paper and assured, "It's okay. We can fix this." I believed him. Why not? He spoke with authority.

So does Christ. To all whose lives feel like a crashed kite, he says, "We can fix this. Let me teach you." Let me teach you how to handle your money, long Mondays, and cranky in-laws. Let me teach you why people fight, death comes, and forgiveness counts. But most of all, let me teach you why on earth you are on this earth.

Don't we need to learn? We know so much, and yet we know so little. The age of information is the age of confusion: much know-how, hardly any know-why. We need answers. Jesus offers them.

But can we trust him? Only one way to know. Do what I did in Rio. Seek him out. Lift up your eyes and set your sights on

Jesus. No passing glances or occasional glimpses. Enroll in his school. "Let me teach you . . ." Make him your polestar, your point of reference. Search the crowded streets and shadow-casting roofs until you spot his face, and then set your sights on him.

You'll find more than a hospital.

You'll find the Only One and Only.

CONCLUSION

AN HONEST PRAYER

"Free flight: Rio de Janeiro to Miami, Florida."

I wasn't the only person to hear about the offer but one of the few to phone and request details. The courier service offered an airline ticket to anyone willing to carry a bag of mail to the States. The deal was tantalizingly simple:

Meet the company representative at the airport, where you'll be given a duffel bag of documents and one ticket. Check the bag when you check in for the flight. Retrieve the bag in Miami before you make your connection. Give it to the uniformed courier representative, who'll await you beyond customs.

No company makes such offers anymore. But this was 1985—years before intense airport security. My dad was dying of ALS, airline tickets expensive, and my checking account as thin as a Paris supermodel. Free ticket? The offer sounded too good to be true.

So I walked away from it.

Many do the same with John 3:16. Millions read the verse. Only a handful trust it. Wary of a catch perhaps? Not needy enough maybe? Cautioned by guarded friends?

I was. Other Rio residents saw the same offer. Some read it and smelled a rat.

"Don't risk it," one warned me. "Better to buy your own ticket."

But I couldn't afford one. Each call to Mom brought worse news.

"He's back in the hospital."

"Unable to breathe without oxygen."

"The doctor says it's time to call hospice."

So I revisited the flyer. Desperation heightened my interest.

Doesn't it always?

When he asks for a divorce or she says, "It's over." When the coroner calls, the kids rebel, or the finances collapse. When desperation typhoons into your world, God's offer of a free flight home demands a second look. John 3:16 morphs from a nice verse to a life vest.

Some of you are wearing it. You can recount the day you put it on. For you, the passage comforts like your favorite blanket:

God so loved . . .

believes in him . . .

shall not perish . . .

eternal life.

These words have kept you company through multiple windswept winters. I pray they warm you through the ones that remain.

Others of you are still studying the flyer. Still pondering the possibility, wrestling with the promise. One day wondering what kind of fool offer this is, the next wondering what kind of fool would turn it down.

I urge you not to. Don't walk away from this one. Who else can get you home? Who else has turned his grave into a changing closet and offered to do the same with yours? Take Jesus's offer. Get on board. You don't want to miss this chance to see your Father.

I didn't. I called the company and signed up. Denalyn drove me to the airport. I found the courier employee, accepted the passage, checked the bag, and took my seat on the plane, smiling like I'd just found a forgotten gift under the Christmas tree.

Do likewise. You don't need to go to the airport, but you do need to make a move. You need to give God your answer: "Christ will live in you as you open the door and invite him in" (Eph. 3:17 MSG). Say yes to him. Your prayer needs no eloquence, just honesty.

Father, I believe you love this world. You gave your one and only Son so I can live forever with you. Apart from you, I die. With you I live. I choose life. I choose you.

If you aren't sure you've told him, you haven't. We can't get on board and not know it. Nor can we get on board and hide it. No stowaways permitted. Christ-followers go public with their belief. We turn from bad behavior to good (repentance). We stop following our passions and salute our new captain (confession). We publicly demonstrate our devotion (baptism).[10]

We don't keep our choice a secret. Why

would we? We're on our way home for Christ's sake.

Thanks to the courier folks, I was present at my father's death.

Thanks to God, he'll be present at yours. He cares too much not to be. Believe in him and you

will . . .

not . . .

perish.

You will have life, eternal life, forever.

NOTES

1. Ker Thun, "Pluto Is Now Just a Number: 134340," MSNBC.com, http://msnbc.msn.com/id/14789691.
2. The Hunger Site, http:/www.thehungersite.com.
3. Os Guinness, *Unspeakable: Facing Up to Evil in an Age of Genocide and Terror* (San Francisco: HarperSanFrancisco, 2005), 4–5.
4. Edward W. Goodrick, ed., John R. Kohlenberger III and James A. Swann, assoc. eds., *Zondervan NIV Exhaustive Concordance*, 2nd ed. (Grand Rapids, MI: Zondervan Publishing House, 1999), 4778, #4742.

5. Stanley Barnes, compiled by, *Sermons on John 3:16*, (Greenville, South Carolina: Ambassador Productions, 1999), 79.
6. Peter Cotterell, *London Bible College Review*, Summer 1989, quoted in Peter Lewis, *The Glory of Christ* (London: Hodder and Stoughton, 1992), 461.
7. Michael Green, *You Must Be Joking: Popular Excuses for Avoiding Jesus Christ* (London: Hodder and Stoughton, 1981), 43, quoted in Lewis, *The Glory of Christ*, 461.
8. Green, *You Must Be Joking*, 43, quoted in Lewis, *The Glory of Christ*, 461.
9. W. E. Vine, *Expository Dictionary of New Testament Words: A Comprehensive Dictionary of the Original Greek Words with Their Precise Meanings for English Readers* (McClean: VA: MacDonald Publishing Company, n.d.), 676.
10. Acts 26:20; Rom. 10:9; Acts 2:38.